FIGHTING FIRE WITH FIRE

Charging Your Way Out Of Credit Card Debt

by

Bob Donnelly

Bloomington, IN  Milton Keynes, UK

authorHOUSE®

AuthorHouse™
1663 Liberty Drive, Suite 200
Bloomington, IN 47403
www.authorhouse.com
Phone: 1-800-839-8640

AuthorHouse™ UK Ltd.
500 Avebury Boulevard
Central Milton Keynes, MK9 2BE
www.authorhouse.co.uk
Phone: 08001974150

First published by AuthorHouse 1/29/2007

ISBN: 978-1-4259-8306-2 (e)
ISBN: 978-1-4259-8307-9 (sc)

Printed in the United States of America
Bloomington, Indiana

This book is printed on acid-free paper.

CAUTION:

Sleeping pills can lead to drug addiction but can be beneficial if taken as directed.

Credit card overuse can lead to greater debt but can actually reduce debt if used as directed!

Introduction

Dear Friend,

Many thanks for your interest in my Jump Start Plan! I'd like to start with a brief explanation of what is being offered.

I am offering you a plan that can allow you to charge down your credit card debt! This Jump Start Plan was developed ideally for those individuals who have already explored alternative means to accomplish the goal of paying down their credit card debt. It assumes that the prospective user of this plan has decided to seek a more suitable and independent strategy to reduce and gain control of his or her debt burden.

In fact, if this Jump Start Plan is followed as stated, it may also benefit those who are not under similar financial constraints but who are seeking to accelerate the pay-off time frame of their debt-load, as well.

In order to effectively utilize this plan and optimize its potential effect on debt reduction, you must already be routinely making at least the minimum monthly payments required by all lenders, and on time. You must also have adequate charging privileges open in each and every account and in amounts equal to or greater than the minimum monthly payment required by that lender.

Basic Rationale of the Plan

1. The suggested credit card charges called for by this plan will not compound one's existing debt.

2. My premise is that you can "fight fire with fire" and is based upon the simple concept that if you charged to create the debt, you can also charge, as a tool, to eliminate the debt. However, this is only possible under a controlled set of rules mandating the exercise of both discipline and restraint. As such, this Jump Start Plan is not to be used or considered by those who are not willing to comply with this important mandate.

3. There is nothing illegal suggested within this plan, nor is there any intent to damage the reputation or financial status of anyone by deception or otherwise. The employment of the underlying principles or strategies within this Jump Start Plan is not meant to be construed as an attempt to undermine the reputation of anyone or organization engaged in the credit card business or other related type business. In fact, this plan was designed to serve as a benefit to both debtor and creditor alike.

4. Once engaged in the Jump Start Plan, there is no commitment of any sort calling for the

sustained use of the plan. Likewise, there is no anticipation of financial hardship or loss factors associated with ceasing to continue with the plan at any given time.

5. The anticipated benefits of utilizing this Jump Start Plan are: the systematic reduction of debt and debt ratios leading to improved credit scores; overall credit-worthiness; and eliminating the necessity of taking on additional loans in order to facilitate the debt pay-down.

6. It should be fully understood that an important objective of this plan is not to induce the individual following it to acquire the habit of over-using credit cards but, conversely, to rely less on the use of credit cards by limiting charges to only those suggested under the Jump Start Plan and in a limited, controlled and focused manner. The ultimate goal is to assist the user in the endeavor to either pay off debt completely or to reduce it to a manageable level. As such, the user is advised to immediately cease to use his/her credit cards for any other purpose until the stated goals have been accomplished.

7. The suggested use of the Jump Start Plan should not be construed as an attempt to discourage anyone from seeking the advice

of an attorney or other reputable individual, professional, or agency.

I hope I have cleared the air and answered most of your questions about the intent of the Jump Start Plan and the potential benefits to be derived from its proper use. You will discover within many cautions that are meant to keep you within the guidelines of the plan's intent, which is **to pay down debt completely or to reduce it to a manageable level.**

As a final introductory note, let's think for a moment about the reason we first made the decision to apply for credit cards. While there may be many, some include: establishing credit, emergency use, and for pure convenience! With that said, wouldn't it be nice to be able to get back to this original intended state? You bet it would!

To borrow a famous quote, "What man can conceive, man can achieve."

So, LET'S GO FOR IT!

Background Story

First of all, I'm quite sure you are wondering who I am and what credentials I might have to develop this plan and render it to you. I'll start by saying what I am not. I'm not a credit card company guru, I'm not a debt counselor, I'm not a Wharton School of Finance Professor, and I'm not a genius. However, I will accept that title, if you later declare me a genius for helping you to solve your perplexing debt problem!

Actually, I'm an independent researcher who developed this Jump Start Plan out of a desire to uncover an alternative solution to the conventional wisdom associated with debt reduction. You might say that I'm one who does not particularly subscribe to the theory that there is merely one way of solving certain types of problems and challenges. I actually took on this challenge to assist a friend who had been drowning in credit card debt.

I'm going to call him "Tom," so I can protect his identity and honor his privacy. It wasn't until

I conducted many hours of research and within some very specific aspects of the financial arena, that I was able to design this simple plan for my friend's utilization. By following my Jump Start Plan, he succeeded in accomplishing his goal of eliminating his overwhelming burden of revolving credit card/charge card debt. Based on his success, I was inspired to render the plan for further distribution.

After all, what a world this would be if those who've discovered useful solutions to everyday problems just harbored the information while witnessing those around them in such desperate need!

My daughter, of whom I am very proud, suggested I write the plan in the most concise manner possible. She seems to think that I enjoy talking a lot! She said, "Dad, cool it with all those philosophical speeches." She sure knows how to call a spade a spade! You know how daughters can get sometimes, right?

Keeping her advice in mind, I want to share the following story about what inspired me to develop the Jump Start Plan.

Tom's Story

Unfortunately, this story I'm about to relate might sound somewhat trite or similar to some of the stories you've probably heard before and have thought to be, in the least, a slight stretch of the imagination. But if you think for a moment, most stories are based on someone's factual events. So, I'm sorry to have to say that this story really does center on a very close friend.

Tom had entered the stock market arena without even a clue and traded in a Bear Market as though it were a Bull Market. At that time, he wasn't aware of the various strategies that could have been employed to trade in that type of environment. (Don't stop reading; this isn't a course on the stock market!)

I didn't know it at the time, but Tom wiped out his life savings. To boot, he used credit card money to pay for margin calls. Sadly enough, he was left with approximately $100,000 in credit card debt, which he struggled desperately to pay down. Unfortunately, he was in lockstep, hardly making any progress by paying only the bare monthly minimum amounts due. In fact, he was totally consumed by it and was living in a state of overwhelming despair.

Prior to this, Tom had a very good credit history and was extended generous credit lines based on his ability to manage his finances within the guidelines established by his creditors. Now isn't this a sad note—for someone who was so financially established, now at middle age, to be experiencing financial devastation and emotional depression. I'm quite sure this sounds a familiar bell to many folks out there these days!

This situation really rocked Tom's world. But it didn't stop there; it created a filtering down effect, impacting loved ones and good friends around him. After all, how would you like to be around a good friend who seemed to have changed 180 degrees in a short period of time? The honest truth is, you just can't help or prevent someone from going downhill if you don't know about the problem. In this case, I personally found out very late in the game.

While most people would choose to remain closed-mouthed when it involves their money management, a sudden downturn of events often triggers the need for emotional support and objectivity. The ideal of holding the line to keep financial matters private quickly becomes wishful thinking. That's how I became involved in Tom's dilemma.

My initial reaction to his problem was a typical sort of knee-jerk reaction, as I blurted out suggestions drawn from the usual spectrum of conventional thinking. I threw in the typical good intentioned stuff that most people are already familiar with. I suggested that he solicit the advice of experts in the field of debt management. Without having any of the real particulars relative to his debt picture, and without first suggesting that he attempt to devise a plan based on his own perspective and self-initiative, I was quoting the commercials and advertisements.

Now, just because he had made some mistakes and was feeling low about the fact hat he had gotten himself into this jam didn't necessarily imply that he was incapable of finding a solution that would emanate from self-reliance. I may have jumped the gun with these suggestions, and in retrospect, I can honestly say that it could have stemmed from daily exposure to the unavoidable, unyielding, subliminal advertising fed to us on the boob tube. Do you remember slogans like, "Winston tastes good like a cigarette should," or "Mmm, mmm good"? I don't wonder why I haven't forgotten them and can still hum them; they were drilled into my subconscious. Yeah, this stuff deliberately serves to weaken one's instinctual tendency to remain silent until a logical understanding of the broader picture is gained. So, maybe the next time I hear a popular jingle, I'll refrain from humming it into my brain!

As a friend who trusted my advice and judgment, Tom responded positively to my suggestions and began to call the advertised companies that boasted their capabilities to reduce anyone's debt by 50% or better. The more he called, the more suspicious he became. They just seemed to make it all sound too good to be true.

When he began his next round of calls, he decided to ask for more specifics, including the qualifications of the firms offering him the most aggressive settlement programs. As he quickly uncovered the lack of governmental regulation of this rather newly emerged industry, he stepped back and took a deep breath. He began to wonder about the legitimacy of the entire industry.

Most of the companies he called advised him that he would need to agree to close his accounts, and that he would have to pay various fees to these companies for their services. Many of these companies required initial and on-going fees for negotiating interest rate reductions with his creditors, including handling of the repayment arrangement that would be filtered through their own office. This made him wonder what might happen to his debt portfolio if the firm itself was to go belly up.

With all the calls he had made, he couldn't seem to find a single company with any credible local or national reputation, not even a franchise with a familiar sounding name or jingle. Watch out for those jingles, folks! Honestly, he wasn't even able to get a recommendation from anyone who had successfully used a debt management firm who was able to handle their debt problem without creating other lasting blemishes on their credit profile.

He now seemed even more confused about what course of action might work best. Sadly, tom was at the point of being able to fork up only the minimum monthly payments, or just a hair more. He was really disheartened and was about ready to pack it all in and file for bankruptcy.

I advised him to hold off on that idea for a while but to remain open to seeking a consultation with a bankruptcy lawyer. I suggested this hold-off since he was still at least current with his obligations. In the interim, I did some scouting around on my own and talked to a few bankers and an attorney on his behalf. Unfortunately, the feedback I received was rather bleak. But I didn't want to pull any punches with Tom, and I didn't want to give him any false hope. As such, I conveyed some of the options to him that included partial consolidation loans mandating that he completely shut down his credit accounts, and then an even more disheartening final resolution: a complicated bankruptcy based upon his unique financial situation.

By the way, one of the bankers figured that if Tom continued paying only the minimum amount due, and based on the combination of interest charges and other related finance charges being assessed, it would take him a whopping 54 years to fully resolve his debt obligations!

The thought of this entire scenario rendered him virtually speechless, and I knew he was devastated. The only thing I could offer at that moment was to treat him to dinner that evening, so that we could regroup and maybe temporarily sidestep the entire issue.

When it came time to pay the dinner bill, I reached into my pocket to get out my wallet. Oh no, it wasn't there! Like a scatterbrain, I'd left it home—cash, credit cards, and all. Wow, of all times to let him down and drop the ball into his court!

Well, I don't have to tell you, it turned out to be the highlight of the evening, and man oh man alive, did it give us a roaring laugh! But true to form, Tom was a really good sport about it and expressed with a positive attitude that although he had a lot of debt, he still relished the fact that he had some charge privileges available on his cards. My friend in need was truly my friend in deed!

But as he took out a credit card and figured in a tip, the silence of the moment sort of stirred something in me. It became clear to me that the fight to keep his credit alive, at least for emergency use, shouldn't end without some sort of major countermove from our end. Now I became more committed than ever to the cause.

NOTES

NOTES

Default by Human Nature

It seems to me that the "humanity" of our human nature somehow relates to our inability to pay more than the stated minimum monthly payment to these credit card bills. I'm quite sure that deeply seated in the psyche of most individuals who are struggling to fork up more than the minimum required monthly payment is the inner struggle of:

"I can't seem to do it regularly or at all! I need to eat, pay for housing, etc., before I allocate more money to reducing my debt. How can I attend that wedding without giving an expected gift? I can't ignore that birthday, that anniversary, that graduation, etc., etc."

Tom also had his set of circumstances. He wasn't able to pay more than the minimum, either! He seemed to have become more and more dependent upon credit as he was losing his shirt in the stock market. He didn't plan it that way, but it happened!

So now, my friends, this is where my Jump Start Plan stands out. This is where I differ from the approach taken by all those well-intentioned financial authors. They continually try to persuade you to re-do your budget as quickly as possible and to become as frugal as possible, all in a good-intentioned attempt to spare you the wrath associated with those high underlying finance charges that are depleting your funds and preventing you from optimizing your future potential.

Those authors are stating what they consider the most rational and well thought-out solutions to the problem, based on the research and experience they choose to bring to the table.

Are they on to something? Sure they are. You know it and I know it. The problem with it is this: You can lead a horse to water, but you can't make him drink. I knew that already, and so did you. When articles are written and directed to a targeted reader, that reader becomes the ultimate judge of whether he or she can follow their advice. That means you! I'm just the observer, trying to help you to figure out where the credit-managing hang up is and how to get you back on track as quickly as possible. I also take the position that no one is a fool.

Now, here's my perspective: It's not an easy task to reverse anyone's mindset in the nick of time! Statistically, the "do as I say or face damnation" approach just isn't working. If it were, why are the rates of defaults and bankruptcies growing out of control? But what if someone (I wonder who that could be?) were to give you a **jump start** by suggesting that you could begin by **charging** to reduce your balances? Maybe it could be the start of something good, a fresh approach that you could handle. I sure think so!

So for those of you who are not quite ready to follow the methodologies as set forth by the noted authors of debt management solutions, I've elected to step out of the box of conventional wisdom by designing a plan that will allow you another opportunistic approach to systematically reduce your debt burden under what I've called the Jump Start Plan.

NOTES

THE JUMP START PLAN

**Charging your way out of credit card debt
Jump-start to freedom from debt**

1. Identification of the Problem: Excessive credit card debt.

2. Examine the Debt: Create a debt chart.

   a. List all credit card accounts by name with the last 4 digits.
   b. List all remaining credit card balances due.
   c. List the APR (Annual Percentage Rate) for each account.
   d. List all the minimum monthly payments due from the most recent statements.
   e. List the payment due date for each account.

3. Solve the Problem: Make charges employing a "snowball" payment strategy.

4. Identify and Utilize: Consider add-on strategies to accelerate the time frame.

5. Final Results: Goal satisfaction, debt reduction, superior credit profile, wisdom!

NOTES

NOTES

Let's Get to Work

Remember, as I said in my introduction, this Jump Start Plan is based on an alternative strategy and is very different from the conventional ones you've often read or heard about. You'll now see how the underlying concept of this plan is based on "fighting fire with fire" by using your credit in a different way.

1. Identify the Problem

For our purposes, we are defining debt as being excessive when you cannot pay down the principal debt and can barely make the monthly minimum payment. Essentially, you are in lockstep with your debt.

2. Examine the Debt

Here is our "working model" of a fictitious shopper's debt load. I want you to create a real debt chart of your own individual credit card debts using this model.

Account	Balance Due/ APR	Minimum Due	Due Date
Visa card 8823	$6,371.87 /21%	$191.15	Oct 5
Store card 4567	$5,243.71 /18%	$157.31	Oct 10
Master Card 3456	$4,657.16/ 15%	$139.71	Oct 25
Visa card 5432	$3,412.32/ 13%	$102.37	Oct 21
Master Card 9876	$2,964.14/ 11%	$ 88.92	Oct 16
Totals:	$22,649.20	$679.46	

Based on the above model, it is apparent that this shopper borrowed, and is under obligation to pay back, a total of $22,649.20.

Likewise, the total of all monthly minimum payments is $679.46.

Throughout the Jump Start Plan, I will continue to refer to this working model; you should be able to identify your own numbers as they relate to the examples I will give going forward.

As a general note, it is advisable to list your credit accounts in order of the ones having the highest APR first. Don't be concerned about the balance amounts not being in a high to low order, or the due dates being out of order. We are striving to first pay down the credit card account charging you the highest interest rate.

3. Solve the Problem—How and What to Charge

This will be our strategy to solve the problem identified as excessive debt. In order to begin solving the problem, we need to go out and start making credit card charges. That's right! I want you to begin to charge the daily goods and services you customarily pay for with cash, debit card, check, or money order. For example, if you ordinarily pay for your grocery shopping with cash, you will now charge it. Likewise, if you've been paying for gasoline and oil changes with your debit card, you'll now begin to charge them. Start using your credit card at the doctor's office, the hair salon, and the dry cleaner. There are numerous other things that you've probably paid for with cash, check, or money order that can also be paid for with a credit card. Below is a partial list to get you started. I'm quite sure you can add to it.

Charging Opportunities:

Supermarket/Grocery
Restaurant
Gasoline/Oil changes
Auto repairs/Car wash/Detailing
Medical/Pharmacy/Eye glasses
Dry Cleaning
Hair salons/Spas

Gyms
Hotels/Motels
Department stores/Specialty stores
Hardware/Home improvement
Computers/Accessories
Pet grooming/Vet/Food

Which card do you use for what?

You can use each card individually to make your various charges. Now here's the Jump Start Plan's special part: you'll use each card **only** up to the same amount as its minimum monthly payment due, as indicated on your monthly statements. For example, if Visa card 8823 has a minimum payment due of $191.15, then you will use this card to make total charges in the amount of $191.15. Please don't exceed this amount.

However, if you must exceed it because you are dealing with odd amounts, do not exceed it by too much. Stay within a few dollars or so. This is important. If you do exceed it, then you will have to add the excess amount to the monthly payment amount. That's okay if you are in a position to pay more than the minimum! But again, charging more than an amount equal to your minimum payment due will not help the cause.

Confused? Okay, let me explain.

Let's say that in the course of a month you would usually go to the supermarket with $190.00 in cash to purchase groceries. (Notice that this amount is very close to one of your minimum monthly payments.) The cash is in your wallet or purse or pocket. However, you also have that credit charge card with you. This means you have the option to either pay cash or to charge your groceries, right?

Under the Jump Start Plan you will charge the groceries. But don't forget, you still have the cash. Remember, I said that you entered the store with cash. Now when you return home, take that cash ($190.00) and put it into a specially marked "snowball" envelope. I'll show you why shortly. Better yet, don't even carry the cash around with you. Leave it at home in the envelope, so you won't be tempted to spend it elsewhere. You could have a trusted relative hold it for you or deposit that cash into a special checking account or savings account that pays interest, at a local bank that doesn't charge big transaction fees or require minimum balances. Preferably, you'll want to keep it away from your usual funds.

NOTE: When I say cash, it also means debit cards, checks, or money orders. If you'd have gotten your cash out of your bank account from an ATM, just leave it in the bank and earmark that sum as your special "snowball" fund.

Can someone else be your charge partner?

If you determine that you need charging help, then yes, you can charge something for another person as long as that other person hands you the cash. It's important to immediately get the cash in your hands so that you don't fall into a collection problem and possibly ruin a friendship or have problems with family members.

As discussed, as long as you use each individual card to make a charge equal to its minimum payment due, it doesn't matter what you purchase or for whom! What matters is that you put aside the cash equivalent, as discussed throughout this plan.

Congratulations! You've just begun to accumulate the extra money needed to pay down your credit card debt. Where did the money come from? It's the cash you would have used to pay for your groceries if I didn't suggest that you charge the groceries!

IMPORTANT: Now that you've charged the groceries, you might be wondering if that charge you've just made was worth doing. You may also be wondering how it makes any sense. You are probably thinking, "Didn't I just increase my credit card debt?"

Let me explain.

We are working with two issues here. On the one hand, you are saving the cash you would have used to pay for the groceries. On the other hand, you have used your charge card to pay for the groceries. Please understand. We are charging the groceries in order to be able to put the cash aside. We need to accumulate cash that will be used in a chunk each month. This chunk that will build up is what I call "the snowball."

The cash will snowball into a large amount and will be used to send in as a substantial payment each month.

About the charge you made:

No problem! Although you used the charge card and it will show up on your next monthly statement as a charge, it will be washed out by the minimum monthly payment you will be making. However, the finance charges you will notice are hardly attributable to this charge. The finance charges apply to the entire outstanding balance. It tags along each month with the debt until the entire outstanding balance is paid off. Just look at some of your older statements. You'll see that the finance charges keep following and building up within the debt. So, if anything, the finance charges attributable to the charge you made will probably be under one dollar, since you are making a similar payment that same month. Don't worry about the pennies. At some point, you will be sending the monthly snowball payment to really make a nice dent in the debt. As such, it will certainly wash out those pennies. It will be like taking a tiny baby step backwards and then... ten giant steps forward! This is the simplistic wonder of the Jump Start Plan!

Based on the model I gave you, Visa card 8823 shows that the model shopper would be charging $191.15, and he would also be making the required minimum payment of $191.15, just as the billing statement calls for. Of course, in your real life situation, the numbers will be different!

Essentially, it's a "wash." Meaning, the payment offsets the charge. Think about it for a moment. I'm sure in your changing days, you must have charged something for, let's say, a hundred dollars and then made a payment that month for a hundred dollars. What you are doing here is actually controlling the amount of the charge. You are structuring the monthly charges to be the same amount as what your statements indicate your minimum monthly payment is.

Some Cautions

Don't take any cash advances and don't charge in excess of the minimum amount we discussed. You can, however, avail yourself of special balance transfer offers, but make sure to read the fine print.

Once again, that model shopper charged $191.15 and then made the minimum monthly payment in the same amount of $191.15. It's a WASH!

The benefit is this: You left the supermarket with the cash you decided not to use. Now remember, I'm not telling you to go out and make crazy charges for things you had no intention of making in the first place. Be careful—make charges only for things that you have the cash for. Don't force yourself to charge things you don't need. You will obviously need groceries, so that's an excellent reason to use the card instead of the cash. This method allows you to save the cash in the envelope.

The cash you are building up is in the same exact amount as the minimum monthly payments you will make. However, you are setting aside this cash until the end of the month, at which time you will have an amount equal to all of your minimum monthly payments.

In the model I gave you, you will note that the total of the minimum payments add up to $679.46. We just reviewed how much cash built up under the model I gave you, but, of course, in real life your actual minimum payments will add up to another amount.

Pat yourself on the back; you are accumulating that hidden treasure to pay down your debt!

You will be accumulating an amount of cash that you never thought existed but will now have available as a significant payment to slam down your debt. You'll first attack the credit card charging you the highest APR. After you successfully pay the first account off, or down to a manageable level, you'll continue on the same course with each and every account.

You will accumulate this money each and every month, and you must use it the same way each month by continuing to send it in a lump sum to pay down your credit card debt. This lump sum is absolutely and unequivocally not to be used for any other purpose. You must understand this fully or you will gain no benefit from the plan and, sadly, you might also wind up in greater debt. So Caveat

Emptor to you! Play by the rules, and you will achieve the stated results.

Back to the Model

In this model, there will be a total of $679.46 in the envelope. Now, once you have your real amount all together, send it off in one lump sum payment to the credit card account that is charging you the highest rate of interest. In this example, the "snowball" of cash would be sent to Visa card 8823, since it has an APR of 21%. We want to "fight fire with fire." They are charging you a high rate of interest, so we want to give them a taste of their own medicine by paying down the high rates first! We will target them first!

How did that first "snowball" payment affect the total remaining balance?

The total balance for Visa card 8823 is $6,371.87, which includes the on-going finance charge build-up we discussed earlier. Therefore, after the "snowball" payment, the next month's balance will be approximately $5,712.41. Remember, the debt snowballed, so we counteract it by throwing our snowball at the debt!

So far, I think you can agree with my introductory statements about the merits of this plan. I'll repeat, we are doing this with no additional loans, no calls to credit card accounts, and no debt counseling, and forget about bankruptcy because progress is in the making!

Clarification of which money is used for what:

What money do you use to make the minimum monthly payments each month? You will use the money you always did to make your other minimum monthly payments. I imagine it came from your pay or some other source, so continue to use your pay as you always have. If you should get some extra funds during the month, such as a bonus or commission or small lottery winning, consider putting some of that in the "snowball" envelope as well.

Remember, don't take money out of the "snowball" envelope. That's not the money to use to pay all the minimums. The money in the envelope is the "snowball" of money hat you will send in a lump sum. Again, it was the cash that you would have used for purchases that you're accumulating.

What Next?

Remember, for each credit card you have, there is a monthly minimum payment that must be met each month. Pay that minimum amount due as soon as you have it available from your pay or other source. Paying it early will also save you money.

Continue to make the minimum payments for your other cards from the source of funds you have always used, NOT from the envelope!

Use the "snowball" money in the envelope to send in a lump sum **only** to the account that is charging you the highest interest.

Each month thereafter continue to charge as instructed and continue to accumulate the money in the envelope. Continue to pay down that card with the highest interest rate (APR) until it Is either paid off completely or is down to an amount that you can manage. The choice is yours!

Then move to the next card, following the same procedure. Soon you will have the next card paid down, and so forth through each of your credit cards.

IMPORTANT: Don't split up the money in the envelope by giving a little to each credit card account unless you have some special reason to do so. Don't melt the "snowball"! Remember, as long as you make the minimum payments to the others, you are considered current and are not in trouble.

4. Add-On Strategy

A little bit you and a little bit me!

We are essentially freezing the balances each month on all but the one card you are targeting for the snowball. When I say "freezing the balances," it's true except for the finance charges that tag along with the debt until the entire balance is fully paid. The one card that is being reduced at a rapid rate is the one that gets the snowball of money thrown at it. However, each will get their turn to get hit with our symbolic snowball! So don't get frustrated with the fact that you will be making great progress on one, while the others are in lockstep.

As you continue to drive down the balance on the card you are targeting, you will note that the minimum payment required will also be less. Don't pay attention to the lower required payment. Continue to put into the snowball envelope the original higher minimum payment amounts that you had when you first started the Jump Start Plan. In other words, the payment that I asked you to write down will remain the same payment you should continue to make on your targeted card. This way, you will be able to build the envelope with the same amount each month. This will help the cause dramatically!

If you were to start to put away in the envelope the new lower minimum due each month, the envelope would have a smaller snowball in it—and you would not be able to rid yourself of the debt, as prescribed. Don't be tempted by their smaller snowball strategy!

There are many other ways to accelerate this Jump Start Plan with a little more effort on your part. For starters, those of you who can afford to send in more than the minimum amount each month, by all means, DO SO! As I mentioned earlier, a bonus, commission, or other money gift could help build the snowball faster too. But do it in combination with this plan. Run some numbers and see how much faster it will bring your balances down.

Take advantage of Balance Transfer opportunities, but read the fine print to make sure it's really a good deal.

In fact, read the fine print to become familiar with all the various service charges that might affect you for different reasons. Try to gain a better understanding of just how finance charges are calculated and the terminology that is used. The more you understand, the better you will be able to gauge your actions.

5. Result—Goal Satisfaction

Stay with the pattern of paying down the worst account with big chunks of money. Your credit report will soon show that you have paid credit cards off or down to a manageable level. This progress may also result in your being awarded higher lines of credit. Take it as a pat on the back but NOT as an opportunity to slip further into debt.

This is what it's all about: eliminating the stress of a heavy debt load while strengthening your credit history in order to avail yourself of future opportunities!

NOTES

NOTES

Summary

This plan was designed to **Jump Start** you into action, so that you can regain control of your out-of-pocket cash flow, structure the charges and payments you make to your credit cards, and get out from under that terrific debt burden. I certainly hope you follow the plan closely, so that it can do just that. But once you get into the swing of it and monitor your steady progress each month, I'm sure that you will devise ways to get it going even faster!

You'll notice that I didn't bug you about drastically cutting down your overall spending. I realize that you might not have been ready to make the sacrifice. But any cutting back you do in your overall spending will certainly be for your own benefit now and in the future. Again, the choice is always yours.

As I stated earlier, the other authors were certainly on to something! So at some point, perhaps when my Jump Start Plan has helped you to feel like you've gotten your head above water, you may want to look closer and explore many of the great ideas they have.

Wishing you all the very best of luck!

Your friend,

Bob Donnelly

About the Author

Bob Donnelly, a third generation native New Yorker, connects much of his personal and professional accomplishments to his early roots-- having grown up in "The Big City."

Born and raised as one of seven children in a struggling family, The Donnelly's lived in the "Yorkville" section of Manhattan in a cramped, (walk-up), tenement apartment house. Living directly across the street and also from a struggling family, was Kit Culkin, one of Bob's earliest childhood friends. While most people immediately associate Kit with his famous son, Macaulay Culkin, --Hollywood's " Home Alone Kid," Bob has a much different connection with Kit.

To Bob, he was an early role model--he was several years older and a true older- brother type. In fact, in his own family, he was the eldest of his siblings and played a parent-like role while he studied unrelentingly in his personal pursuit to achieve Hollywood fame. Kit radiated a positive and "can do" attitude to others around him and served as a true early example of-- "Tough Individualism."

Back in the day, the struggle was all about overcoming adversities such as poverty, limited job opportunities, and in general--the prospect of an uncertain future. Many of these issues-- as perplexing as they seemed, were actually dealt with at the kitchen table-and in a family consensus fashion.

Out of shear necessity, most folks maintained a —"Just keep it simple," attitude.

For example, if you needed food/you needed to seek work, if you had a loose tooth/you may have looked for a piece of string and the nearest doorknob, and if you needed a new outfit/you looked in your sibling's closet. The times called for a great deal of resourcefulness and self-sufficiency, to say the least.

Remaining ever cognizant of these fundamental lessons in self preservation, Bob would later recoil this basic native intelligence by associative reasoning, into a more refined problem solving "Model," later to be used in his entrepreneurial endeavors. Bob has a profound passion for applying simple logic to uncover simple solutions. He also subscribes to the notion that, "What man can conceive, man can achieve."

Bob's professional background dates back to 1968 when he entered banking- enjoying a lengthy career in economics/statistical research, real estate appraising, brokerage and management. In 1975, he was awarded a B.B.A Degree from Pace University, NYC, while also serving as a Sergeant in the New York National Guard. During his career as an analyst and researcher, he developed a tremendous fascination for "fact-finding." This undeniable recognition served as the catalyst, influencing his decision to branch out on his own-- to gain the freedom to embark upon his more creative goals and ambitions.

In 2001, he was awarded his first US Patent for a rather simple gadget-- benefiting tradesmen. While continuing along the creative path, he serves as a freelance --business/ article writer for a local newspaper. In April of 2006, Bob appeared on the CNN Cable TV Show, "Open House" --in an Episode ("Small Spaces") centering on a (home makeover) -- renovation project. Using hands-on skills, he worked along with the highly acclaimed, Stephen Saint-Onge, who is regarded as one of the top ten Professional Interior Designers in the country.